FUN-TASTIC FACTS!

Learning Drums For Beginners Kids

CRASH THE CYMBALS, BASH THE SNARE, BECOME A DRUMMING SUPERSTAR!

INTRODUCTION

Boom! Bash! Ready to Rock with Drums?

Hey there, young drumming dynamo! Have you ever felt a beat pulsing in your chest, a rhythm tapping your toes? Does the sound of pounding drums make you want to jump up and groove? Then this book is for you!

Welcome to the amazing world of drums! Here, you'll embark on a wild adventure where you'll learn the secrets of this awesome instrument. We'll be exploring the different parts of a drum set, transforming our hands into drumming machines, and most importantly, having tons of FUN creating our own music!

This book is your personal guide to becoming a drumming superstar. It's packed with clear instructions, cool pictures, and step-by-step lessons that make learning easy and exciting. So grab your drumsticks, get ready to rock, and let's turn that inner rhythm into a powerful beat!

TABLE OF CONTENTS

TABLE OF CONTENTS

LET'S START

I love to see the excitement in a child when they decide they want to do something new...like taking up drumming. I have a young son myself and he loves drumming. I taught him a whole summer of lessons and now he thinks he knows it all! Ha! But, there are a few things that I was able to set him up with so he had the right tools to start learning.

I'm going to go over everything your child would need to get started in drums or percussion. This would cover drum sets, sticks, lessons, books, pads, metronomes, etc. I am specifically writing this for my own new students but I know this will help other parents too. This article covers kids from ages 5-10. If they are older, take a look at my other article that covers ages 10 to adult: Definitive Drum Practice Guide from Beginner to Advanced - Part 1 - Scheduling and Gear.

What Age Should They Start?

I always say that the age of five is probably the youngest a child could start learning drums. Of course, that depends on how much they are able to focus. Some kids at 5 years old can't focus at all while some can focus for at least 20-30 minutes. This is a relatively normal attention span with how most kids develop. My son didn't try lessons until he was 6 and it was a struggle for him to focus longer than 10 minutes. It would be safe to say that any child 8 years old and up would be ready to start learning drums.

Should They Get Lessons?

I have an opinion about "lessons vs. self-taught" that I would like to explain so I can help you decide on whether they should get lessons or not.

When you self-teach, in any subject or discipline, it only takes you longer to reach your goals if you do it without the direction of a teacher that has already reached similar goals. I understand that everyone learns a bit differently, but as long as you have a good teacher, they will always find a solution faster than you can. Otherwise you're just taking shots in the dark to try to figure out techniques, licks, etc.

Bottom line is, good teachers will always help you reach your goals faster. At a younger age (younger than 12), it is almost imperative to get them lessons. There aren't a lot of children that would be able to learn drumming without some direction to start with.

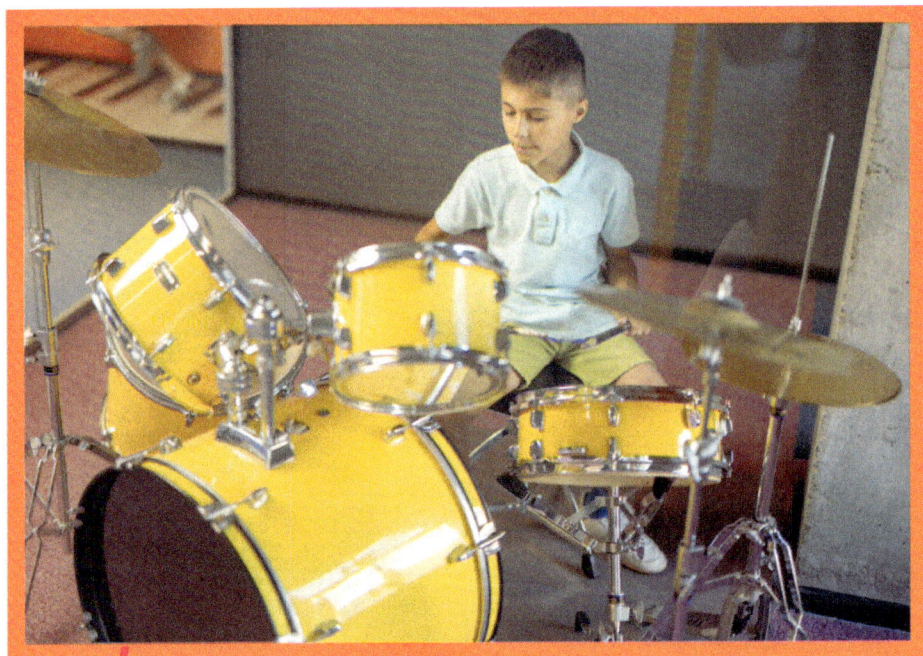

HOW TO BUY YOUR FIRST DRUM SET

The drummer is the heartbeat of any band, and they also own more pieces of gear than anyone else in the group. The good news is that you don't need to own it all from day one. Buying a drum kit for a beginning student can be overwhelming, so we've broken down what you need to know, from the types of kits to consider for a beginner to essential hardware that's required to play the songs that will keep your student motivated.

SHOPPING FOR A BEGINNER DRUM SET

The right place to start drum shopping depends on the person you're shopping for. You'll want to consider the age of the drummer, their eagerness to learn, where and when they will practice at home, and the budget you're working with.

Unlike most other instruments, drums can be arranged in different ways and customized to the drummer's style or preferences.

A beginning drummer's kit or kid's drum set should look quite different from a veteran drummer's. A kit for a beginning drummer should provide what they need to build fundamental skills without adding in hardware or pieces that only distract the student.

WHAT TO LOOK FOR WHEN BUYING DRUMS

If cost is your main concern and you're shopping for a kid's drum set for your student, you can find something inexpensive for her/him to bang around on. The least expensive option is an all inclusive bundle, but you'll want to verify what's included in the package.

A drum set needs shells (the actual drums), cymbal stands, cymbals, bass drum pedal and a throne to be fully functional.

BEST DRUM SETS FOR KIDS

If your beginning drummer is younger than eleven or twelve years old, they may have trouble reaching and playing everything on an adult sized drum kit. Manufacturers make junior sized kits where drum diameters have been scaled down to allow younger kids to reach all drums and kick pedals.

Make sure to try out any kit before you buy to make sure reach and size aren't a problem. Avoid kits that are available in toy stores unless your child is five or younger. These may look like real kits, but the drums are likely plastic and they are little more than toys.

Most major drum makers sell junior kits or "pocket kits" that are appropriately sized for younger drummers. Your child will eventually outgrow a junior kit, but not quickly.

WHAT DRUM SETS ARE GOOD FOR KIDS?

A junior kit can be set up differently as your student grows and you can expect them to play it until they're twelve or so, depending on their size.

Here are some models we suggest for those who are not quite big enough for a full-size kit:

- Ludwig Junior
- Gammon 5-Piece Junior
- Rise by Sawtooth

BEST BEGINNER DRUM SETS FOR ADULTS

Major manufacturers make some kits that have great tone and that also fit the budget of an adult beginning drummer. We suggest you take a look at the following models:

- Pearl Roadshow
- Pearl Export
- Gammon 5 Piece
- Tama Imperialstar
- Gretsch Catalina

BUYING DRUMS ONLINE

If you're shopping online, be sure to read the list of what's included. Some of these sets have more in the online photo than actually ships with the set.

Consider price and quality. Like most things, the quality of the drum set will determine the cost. The least expensive all in one sets come with a couple of warnings.

The shells will be usable, but the cymbals and hardware will likely be a little flimsy, probably needing to be replaced in the near future if the kit gets regular use. But if what you're looking for is a mix of toy and instrument, maybe this is the right choice.

Research the drum hardware. Take a look at the hardware and make sure it looks solid. If you're shopping online, you can zoom in on the images of the gear for a closer. Each of the three legs on the cymbal stands should be made of two pieces.

If each leg is "one-ply", so to speak, or the pieces that loosen and tighten look like standard hardware store wing nuts, you're probably going to have to replace that stand sooner than later.

Look for bundled hardware. You can also find bundled hardware and cymbal sets that tend to be less expensive than buying pieces separately. Pay close attention to the images and descriptions of the hardware if you're buying online and don't get anything "one-ply."

BUYING DRUMS IN PERSON

If buying drums for a young person, you will want to make sure they sit behind the kit and try to reach all components. Once you've determined that they can reach everything, determine what kind of adjustments can be made as your student grows.

If you're trying to decide between multiple kits, you should listen to them being played at full force. If you or your student are a beginner, ask the salesperson if anyone in the store can play the full kit. Most music stores are staffed by musicians, so this shouldn't be a problem. Compare the overall tone of the kits to determine what you like best, and keep your preferred style of music in mind.

You will likely be purchasing the model that has been on display, so examine it closely for any damaged heads, cracked cymbals, or scratches in the wood or finish of the drum shells.

PRO TIP: TRANSPORTING DRUMS
Transporting drums requires a lot of space, so make sure you are prepared to take them with you and have a place prepared to set them up at home. The store will also have drum cases for sale, but this will add to the overall cost and may not be necessary unless the drums are being moved a lot.

BUYING A NEW VS. USED DRUM KIT

For beginners, should you buy new or used? While used drum sets can offer significant savings, first time buyers may be overwhelmed by the options and choices. New kits offer many advantages including warranties and you know that the kit has not been abused.

New kits are probably a better option for the first time buyer, but if you have a drummer friend that is willing to help you with checking out the used kits, it may be worth the effort.

BUYING A NEW BEGINNER OR KID'S DRUM KIT

There are a lot of options for shell packs that will get you a set of drums without hardware or cymbals. You'll get a broader range of brand and aesthetic options this way, and most brands and models should be totally decent.

To find the best drum brands for your kid, it's always wise to read up on the reputation of the brand and find any reviews of the specific product you're looking at. There will likely be more than one option at each price point, so choose something with a good reputation that your kid will think is cool.

1. SELECTING A KID'S DRUM KIT THAT YOUR CHILD IS EXCITED ABOUT

One of the big concepts at School of Rock is that if we help our students love playing their instruments, they get better that much faster. Having a set of drums that looks cool and excites your kid's interest can make it that much more fun to sit down and play.

2. BUY DRUM HARDWARE UPFRONT

If you're shopping in person, the salesperson will tell you that it will save you money, in the long run, to buy decent hardware up front, and they're right. For cymbals, make sure you're getting something name-brand. Zildjian, Paiste, and Meinl are some of the better-known names, but not the only good ones.

3. LOOK FOR ALL-INCLUSIVE DRUM KITS

The second tier of all-inclusive kits can be pretty decent and will save you from having to assemble a set from a la carte pieces. Just like the big guitar brands have affordable sub-brands, the big names in drums have entry-level models that are usually quality.

Many of the mid-range kits that include shells and hardware

don't include cymbals or a throne, so be sure to look at that before you make a final decision.

If cymbals are included, make sure there's a brand name on them – you don't want cymbals no one is willing to claim. If you end up deciding to buy cymbals separately, there are loads of options – more info below.

4. SELECT THE BEST DRUM KIT FOR YOUR NEEDS

Most major drum companies produce great beginner kits. It is generally recommended that you stick to the best-known drum brands: Ludwig, Tama, Pearl, Slingerland, Sonor, DW/PDP, Gretsch, and Mapex are all trusted brands.

BUYING A USED BEGINNER OR KID'S DRUM KIT

Drums, cymbals, and hardware don't tend to lose quality with use unless they're mistreated, and you can find nice gear at a good price shopping for used gear. Most instrument stores will have used gear, and if you're in a shop with a good reputation you can feel pretty confident you're getting something in good condition.

HOW TO INSPECT USED DRUM EQUIPMENT

You can also find good pieces from private sellers, just look closely at each piece. Here are some things to watch out for with used drum gear.

- **Shells.** Look closely at the shells for any cracks or missing hardware. Little screws and nuts can be replaced if the drum is sound, but if you're not getting a great deal it's probably not worth replacing little parts. It's likely that used drums will need new heads (the parts that you hit). It's not difficult to change the heads on a drum set, but it's another potential cost to take into account.
- **Hardware.** For hardware, make sure none of the pieces that tighten and loosen are stripped and none of the pieces that should be straight are bent. Cymbal stands should have two felt discs for the cymbal to sit between and a piece to hold that all in place on the stand. Usually that top fastener screws down on top of the upper piece of felt, though some newer designs you can just pinch to release.

- **Cymbals.** Looking at used cymbals, every crack, no matter how small, will grow over time. Any crack in a cymbal you're considering buying is a sign to pass. Sometimes little cracks can appear along the circular grooves of a cymbal and be easy to miss, so look closely for that.

If the hole at the center of the cymbal is not a perfect circle, it's a sign of stress on the cymbal probably due to not being fastened on the stand properly. Also look for little cracks around the center hole as a sign of damage that will quickly lead to the cymbal sounding bad and being unusable.

TYPES OF DRUM KITS

The drum is one of the simplest musical instruments ever invented, but since the introduction of synthesizers in the 70s and 80s, drummers have had the option of computerized electronic drums that can produce a wide range of sounds. Even if you decide to go with traditional acoustic drums, there are two types of drum kits to choose from.

Many manufacturers produce each kit they make in two different configurations, fusion and standard. Fusion kits have toms with smaller diameters that produce a sharp punchy tone. But standard kits are best for rock. The larger tom diameters produce more volume and have a larger tone that mixes well with electric guitars.

CHOOSING AN ACOUSTIC DRUM SET VS. AN ELECTRONIC DRUM SET

There are two types of drum sets, traditional (acoustic) drums versus electronic drums. There are advantages to each type of drum.

TRADITIONAL (ACOUSTIC) DRUM KITS FOR BEGINNERS

Acoustic drums have metal cymbals and use wood and metal drums that are designed to project sound. Traditional drums have a better "feel" and are less complicated to set up.

WHAT IS AN ELECTRONIC DRUM SET?

Electric drum kits have rubber pads that when hit send sounds to either an amplifier or to headphones. For this reason, they have the ability to reduce or eliminate the volume of the drums. For students living in apartments or anywhere where sound levels are a concern, electronic drums in a kid's drum set are a great solution.

WOOD USED FOR DRUM SHELLS

BIRCH
Loud drum
Balanced sound
Good for recording

BUBINGA
Exotic wood
Punchy notes
Mid-range sound

MAHOGANY
Warm/darker sound
Most rare type

MAPLE
Warm/bright tones
Highly-versatile

Many entry level drums are made of less expensive woods such as POPLAR.

DRUM HARDWARE INCLUDES:

Drum Hardware

Drum & cymbal stands/rack

Cymbals

Snare and tom drums

Drum heads

Bass drum pedals

Drum thrones

Drumsticks & brushes

- **Drum & cymbal stands/racks**. Cymbals and some types of drums have their own stands. These are adjustable and allow the drummer to position the parts of the kits exactly where they want them. "Rack" systems integrate the functions of several stands, these can be useful for elaborate kits with multiple drums and cymbals.
- **Cymbals.** There are three main types of cymbals: crash, ride, and hi-hats. The crash cymbals are used to accent songs while the ride cymbal tends to be a large, thick cymbal that produces a bell-like tone. The hi-hats are a pair of smaller thin cymbals that are activated by a foot pedal that makes them strike each other. The foot pedal is included with the hi-hat stand and does not need to be purchased separately. The hi-hats are also played with the sticks.
- **Snare and Tom drums.** The snare drum is the loudest and most prominent drum. The bottom, or resonate, drum head has a system of "snares" or thin wires that gives the drum its sharp sound. Generally, a drum kit will have three tom drums - a floor tom mounted on a stand, as well as a medium and high tom mounted to the set itself.
- **Drum heads.** All drums have heads, which will generally be included in your purchase. The top head (the one that is struck) is called a batter head and the other bottom head is called the resonant head. The heads are tuned with a system of "lugs" that circle the drum. Bass drum pedals. Bass drum pedals are used to play the bass or "kick" drum. There are two types of bass drum pedals: single and double. It is recommended that beginners start with a single pedal.
- **Drum thrones.** The throne is the name of the drummer's seat. The drum throne should be adjustable and comfortable, with the entire drum kit set up around it.

- **Drumsticks & brushes.** Drumsticks are a very important part of the drummer's sound. They come in different sizes and are made from different types of wood. The size of the stick and the type of tip (which can be wooden or plastic) produce different tones. Brushes are sticks that have fan-like metal or plastic brushes on the end. These produce a much softer, quieter sound.

FOUND YOUR PERFECT DRUM SET? YOU'RE READY TO JAM.

The last thing you want, once you've picked out the best beginner drum set for your kid, is to have it sit untouched for the rest of her/his childhood. At School of Rock, we focus on teaching students to enjoy playing their instrument first and build the broader concepts of music on top of that foundation, using performance as the motivation and the payoff.

When students know that they're going to walk out on stage in a real rock venue and play a legit concert, the practicing tends to take care of itself.

We would love for your child to have all of the pieces in place the second they get their instrument – guitar lessons, bass lessons, a beginner or intermediate/advanced winter day camp, and a concert to start rehearsing for.

At School of Rock, we take total beginners and within a few short months have them performing on stage, going on tour, building confidence, and making lifelong memories and friendships with kids that love the same things they do.

HOW TO SET UP A DRUM SET

Experienced drummers know that how you arrange your drum kit has a direct effect on how you play and what you can do. However, learning how to set up your drum kit can be as challenging as actually playing, especially for beginner drummers!

HOW TO SET UP A DRUM SET

When setting up your drum set, you'll want to change how you arrange your drums based on the number of pieces you're dealing with. Typically, most beginners start with a 4-piece or 5-piece drum setup, but many musicians add additional components to their as their skills improve.

1. Identify the 3 main parts of your drum kit

Most beginner drum sets have three main components: drums, hardware and cymbals.

- Drums. Most drum sets typically include the bass (or kick) drum, the snare drum and toms.
- Hardware. Common drum hardware includes the bass drum pedal, the throne, and the hi-hat and cymbal stands.
- Cymbals. Different types of cymbals include the crash, the ride and the hi-hats.

2. SET UP YOUR BASS DRUM

Place your bass or kick drum so that it's at the center of your drum kit. Note that your bass drum has adjustable legs. These are used to anchor your bass drum to the floor so it doesn't move around as you play.

For this reason, it's important to adjust the legs so they are

Parts of a 5-Piece Drum Setup

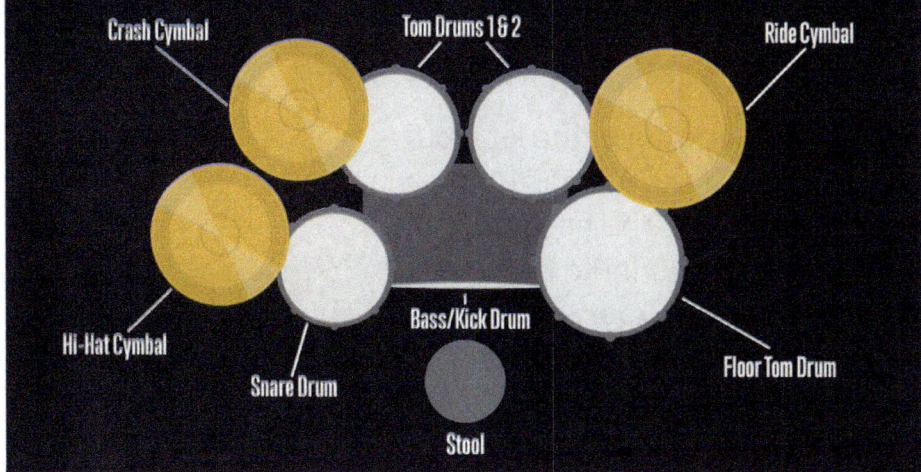

Crash Cymbal
Tom Drums 1 & 2
Ride Cymbal
Hi-Hat Cymbal
Bass/Kick Drum
Floor Tom Drum
Snare Drum
Stool

equal on both sides, since unequal legs will cause your drum set to wobble during play. Check the tips of the legs on your bass drum to make sure they dig into the floor and prevent your drum from sliding around.

3. ADJUST YOUR BASS DRUM PEDAL

When setting up your drum set for the first time, pay special attention to the bass pedal. You can find the bass drum pedal attached to the hoop of your bass drum. As you step on the pedal, the beater should strike the bass drum head in the middle of your drum and then bounce back.

If stepping on the pedal is too hard or makes your legs tired, then you'll need to adjust the action or tension of the bass pedal to make it less tight. If the pedal stays on the drum head and does not bounce back, then the tension is too loose.

If the tension is too loose, you'll need to adjust the tension to be tighter so the drum head springs back. Most pedals have a knob or screw that you can turn to control the tension, but this may be different depending on your model.

4. PLACE YOUR SNARE DRUM

As you arrange your drum kit, you will need to adjust the height of your snare drum. The height of your snare drum should be set a few inches above your leg and set so you can easily hit the drum with either of your hands without hitting the rim of your drum.
Set up your drum so your snare throw-off, the lever that engages the snare, is on the left-hand side of your drum. Most drummers set up their snares flat, although traditional players sometimes set their drums so that it slightly tilts down and away.

5. SET UP YOUR TOMS

Most drum sets have two types of toms: floor toms and mounted toms. Your floor toms should be set so it is roughly the same height as your snare drum, while your mounted tom (or toms) should be set up at a slight angle towards you. The arrangement of your toms can be changed to make it easier to play. For drum arrangements with more than one mounted tom, you can place your toms so they are a few inches apart and sit at equal angles.
If it's uncomfortable to hit your floor tom, try angling the tom slightly toward you. You may find that angling your toms

will be more comfortable than setting them up completely flat, although this can vary depending on the height of your drum throne.

6. PLACE YOUR DRUM THRONE

The drum throne is where you will sit as you play. For increased playability, place your drum throne in a spot where you can reach all components of your drum set. This will allow you to play with the least effort and help you prevent injury.

7. SET UP YOUR HI-HAT

When sitting at your drum set, the positioning of your hi-hat should be just to the left of your snare. You attach hi-hat cymbals to the rod of your stand using a clutch that secures the top cymbal to the rod. This allows you to open and close the hi-hats. Make sure that the pedal for your hi-hat is in a position where your foot can comfortably reach it.

It's important that your hi-hat cymbals sit higher than your snare. Setting your hi-hats to the same height as your snare, or lower, might make it harder to hit.

8. ARRANGE YOUR CRASH AND RIDE CYMBALS

Typically, most drummers use one or two crash cymbals and one ride cymbal. Your ride cymbal should be set up to your right, usually just over the floor tom.

If you're using one crash cymbal, set it up to the left of your kit somewhere between your snare drum and your mounted tom.

If you're using a second crash cymbal, you should place it between your mounted tom and your floor tom. Make sure both crash cymbals sit a few inches above the mounted toms, but not too high. You'll want to keep them within a comfortable reach.

HOW TO SIT WITH PROPER DRUM SET POSTURE

Now that you have your kit set up, let's talk about the correct posture for drumming. Maintaining proper drum set posture is important because it will help you play more efficiently, improve your sound and decrease your risk of injury.

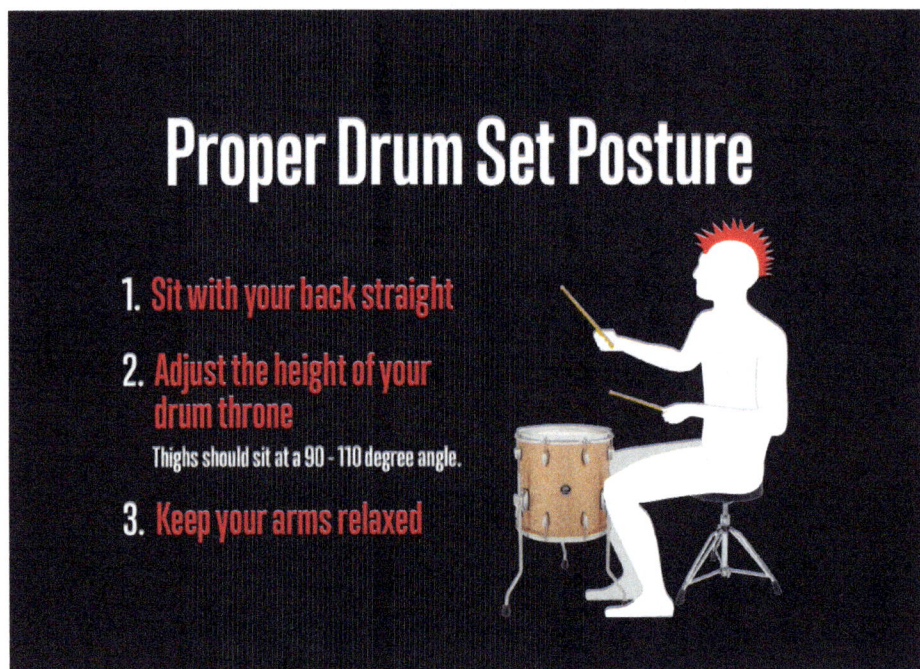

Proper Drum Set Posture

1. Sit with your back straight

2. Adjust the height of your drum throne
   Thighs should sit at a 90 - 110 degree angle.

3. Keep your arms relaxed

- **Sit with your back straight.** When playing your drum kit, keep your back straight. Don't slouch forward since this puts pressure on your lower back and can cause injury. Watching videos or live performances of professional drummers can help beginners visualize proper posture. If sitting up straight is too difficult, some drum thrones come with a built-in back for additional support as you play.

- Adjust the height of your drum throne. For good posture, adjust the height of your drum throne so your thighs sit at a 90 to 110 degree angle. Setting your drum throne too high or too low will make it harder to play your bass drum, and will make your legs get tired.
- Keep your arms relaxed. When playing the drums, keep your arms close to your sides with your elbows tucked in. This will help you maintain a good drum stroke that produces a good tone. Raising your arms any higher may cause your strokes to sound pushed or forced.

HOW TO HOLD DRUMSTICKS WITH PROPER GRIP

No matter what type of grip you use to hold your drumsticks, your grip should be relaxed and your thumbs should be facing upward. This will give your sticks a proper bounce when they strike the drum heads and result in a better sound.

TRADITIONAL GRIP VERSUS MATCHED GRIP

There are two main types of grips: traditional and matched.

Traditional Grip
Right hand holds drumstick overhand, and left hand holds drumstick underhand.

TRADITIONAL DRUMSTICK GRIP

In traditional grip, your right hand holds the stick in an overhand fashion. Your left hand holds the stick in an underhand fashion with the stick resting between the middle and ring fingers. Marching bands and jazz drummers often hold their drumsticks this way.

MATCHED DRUMSTICK GRIP

For matched grip, hold both of your drumsticks overhand between your thumb and index finger. There are three variations of the matched grip: American, French and German.

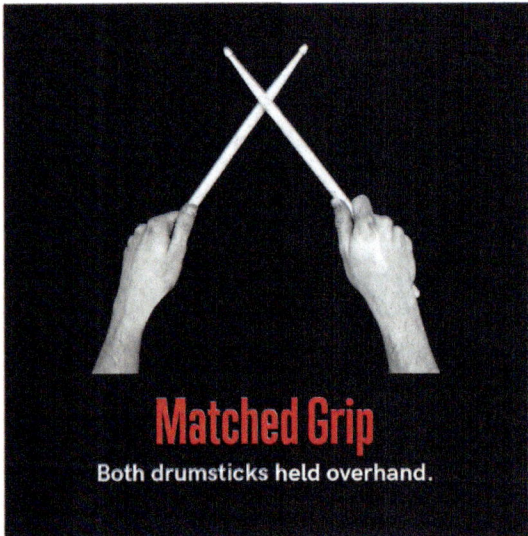

Matched Grip
Both drumsticks held overhand.

Variations of Matched Grip

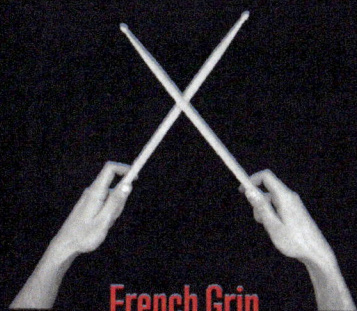

French Grip
Palms face each other and drumsticks are controlled mostly by fingers.

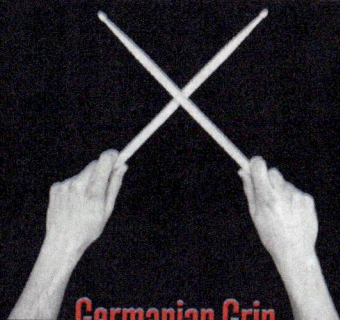

Germanian Grip
Both palms down to face the drum head.

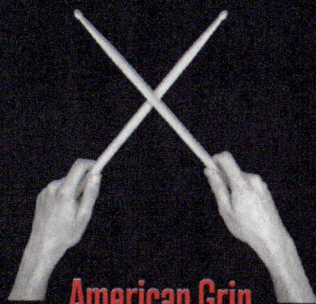

American Grip
Palms sit at a roughly 45 degree angle to the drum.

French grip. When using the French grip, your palms face each other and the stick is controlled mostly by your fingers. This drumstick grip allows you to play with more finesse and control.

Germanian grip. The Germanian or German grip has the palms down to face the drum head. This gives you a strong, powerful stroke that is controlled mostly by the wrist. This is the grip used during the Moeller technique which involves a whipping motion of the wrist.

American grip. The American grip is a hybrid of both the French and German grip. With this drumstick grip, your palms should sit at a roughly 45 degree angle to the drum. This gives you the finesse of the French grip and the power of the German grip.

No matter which grip you use, maintaining great posture and properly setting up your kit can help you play better, sound better and avoid injury.

Parts of the drum

This is the anatomy of a tom:

These are the parts of a snare drum (the one on the right has been turned upside down):

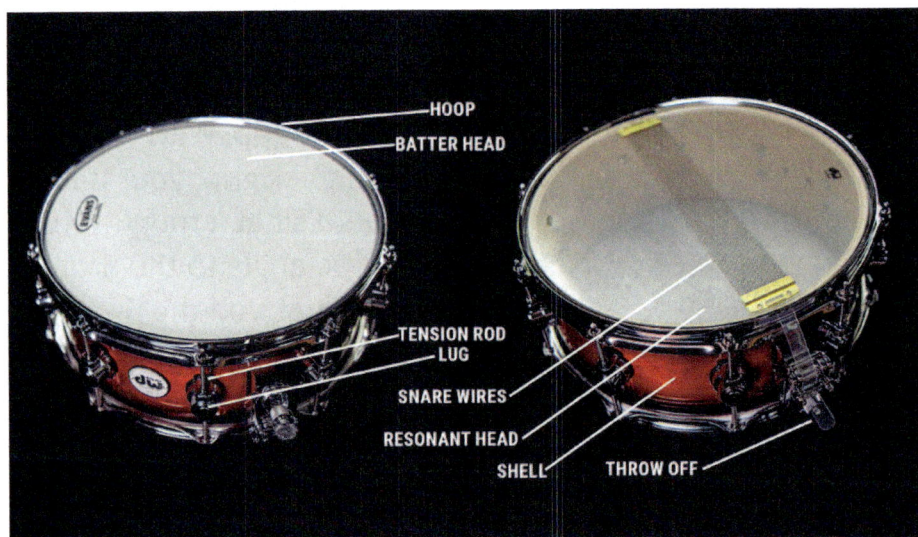

DRUM NOTATION & SHEET MUSIC: HOW TO READ IT

As a starting drummer, it is helpful to read drum sheet music because it will allow you to learn and remember new songs without having to guess by ear or remember every stroke you make.

Drum notation is how we write down and convey patterns, rhythms, and songs from one drummer to another. It is, in many ways, the language of drummers. As a starting drummer, it is helpful to read drum sheet music because it will allow you to learn and remember new songs without having to guess by ear or remember every stroke you make. Drum notation will also help you during the start of your drumming career, as you can simply read to complex rhythms and techniques, which you can revisit and practice just by taking our your sheet music. Drum sheet music can massively improve your timing, control, and understanding of drums.

Finally, the most advanced drummers can still use drum notation to study new songs quickly and write their own rhythms to remember them at any time.

This guide will cover the specifics of drum notation, accents, and general music notation.

WHY READ SHEET MUSIC?

Reading drum sheet music is the perfect way to practice drums uniformly, master different drum skills, learn drum techniques and teach yourself your favorite songs. It's not just for beginner drummers.

The Fear of Reading Sheet Music

The idea of reading drum notationmay strike fear in the beginner drummer, but drum notation is just a little different from standard sheet music, as well as easier to read. Drum notation can be great if you get into session drumming and you need to be able to learn a song quickly.

If limb coordination is still getting you down, you can check out this free course on Limb Independence from Gabe.

THE BASICS OF DRUM NOTATION

Drum notation is a little like music notation. It's a musical language written on music manuscripts, the same as sheet music. But, instead of the symbols representing a musical note,each symbol on the drum notation represents a different part of the drum kit.

Reading drum sheet music will help you bring your uncoordinated limbs back into focus and make you a more solid drummer with excellent timing and regular rhythm.

How to Read Drum Notation

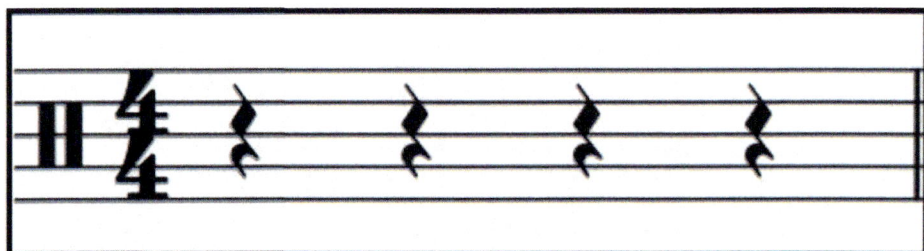

A music staff is made up of five horizontal black lines, containing four white spaces. This empty staff shows one measure of four beats, where each beat is a rest.

A music staff is made up of five horizontal black lines, containing four white spaces. This empty staff shows one measure of four beats, where each beat is a rest.

Reading drum sheet music is like reading a book: from left to right and line by line, top to bottom. The staff is made up of five lines and four spaces across. Each line and space is called a staff line and has a number, ranging from staff line 0 (the highest black line) and staff line 1 (the highest white space) to staff line 8 (the lowest black line). Notes can be positioned on the lines and spaces as well as above and below the staff, on 'invisible' staff lines such as staff line -2 or staff line 9.

In drum notation, each note represents a different part of the drum kit and each one has a specified place on the staff, making it easier when reading. Drum notes can be at the same horizontal point on the staff, but they'll be either above or below the other notes.

Breaking it down further,drums are represented by dots, whereascymbals are represented by an X. Both have stems attached like sheet music notes. This makes reading the notation easier, enabling you to pick the difference between drums and cymbals, even if you're sight-reading.

Standard Drum Notation

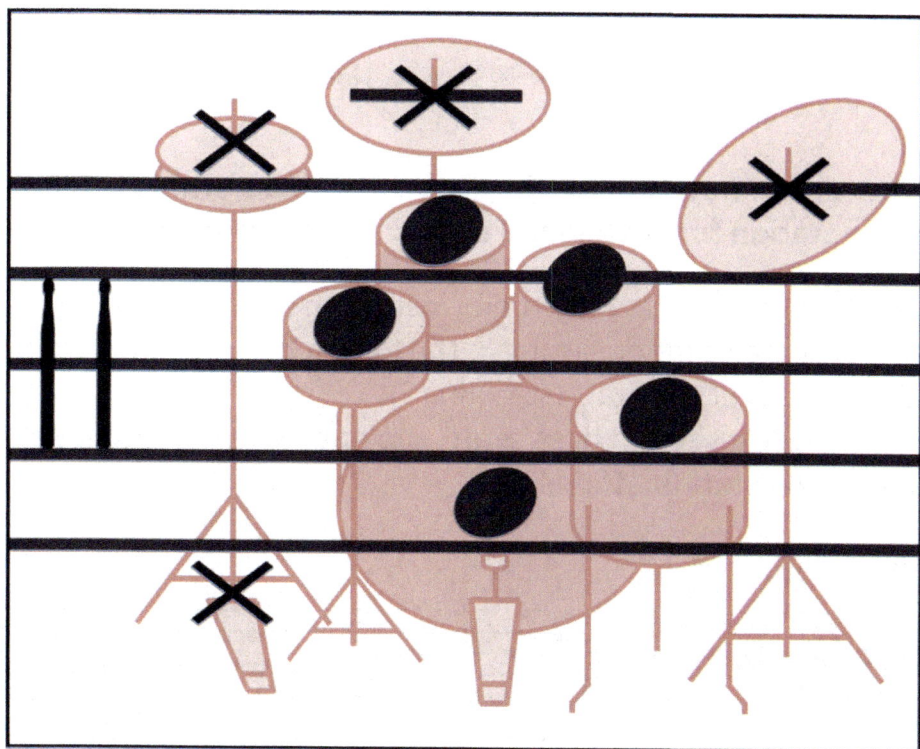

This overview shows what part of the drum a symbol represents and whereabouts it sits on the staff. It is helpful to imagine the symbols on the staff line corresponding to the relative height of the drums and cymbals on your drum kit. Working out what each note means will become second nature as you practice working with drum notation.

Let's look at the drum notation for a standard four- or five-piece kit and some less commonly used notations for extra pieces. The guide is written in order of where the symbols are located on the staff, starting from the bottom.

Bass Drum or Kick Drum

Bass drum 1   Bass drum 2

The regular notation for the bass drum (bass drum 1), and the notation for the second bass drum if you use one.

The bass drum is usually thelowest drum of a typical drum kit, with the notation sitting in the lowest or first space from the bottom of the staff (staff line 7).

If you have a second bass drum, the notation is on the lowest line of the staff (staff line 8).

Floor Tom

Floor tom   Other low toms

36

The regular notation for the floor tom, and alternative notations for other lower-registered toms.

Floor toms or low toms tend to be the next lowest drum in the kit, so the floor tom notation is situated on the second space from the bottom of the staff (staff line 5).
Other lower-registered toms sit on the lines above (staff line 4) and below (staff line 6) this tom with the same style of notation.

Snare Drum

Snare drum

The notation for the snare drum.

Up next we have the snare drum. Thebeating heart of the drum kit sits on the second space on the staff (staff line 3). Like the Bass drum and floor tom, the snare drum is represented as a dot with a stem.

Tom 1 and Tom 2

Tom 1   Tom 2

The notation for the high tom (tom 1) and mid tom (tom 2).

The high tom is located in the top space of the staff (staff line 1), and the mid tom right below that space, on the line (staff line 2).

Hi-Hats

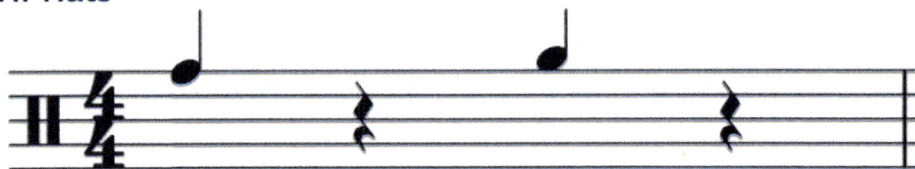

[Additional toms]

The notation for additional toms your drum set may include.

Depending on the type of drum set you're playing, you may or may not have both a high and mid tom available. Additional toms below the typical tom 1, or high tom, and tom 2, or mid tom, are placed on the first line from the top (staff line 0) or right above it (staff line -1).

Hi-hat   Hi-hat pedal

The regular hi-hat notation as well as the pedal hi-hat.

Usually situated above the top line (staff line -1), the hi-hat has several different variations of notation on drum sheet music.
The hi-hat is notated using an X, as it is a cymbal, with a stem. The regular hi-hat notation is located above the top

line (staff line -1). The hi-hat pedal notation is sat underneath the bottom line, below the bass drum notation, and is represented as an X with a stem as well.

Ride Cymbal

Open hi-hat   Closed hi-hat

The notation for an open hi-hat and a closed hi-hat.

In addition, articulation symbols can be used to denote how the hi-hat should be played. A small 'o' above the hi-hat note indicates the hi-hat should be open, whereas a small '+' means the hi-hat should be closed. Several more notations indicate more unusual articulations, such as a loose hi-hat (ø) and open/close (o+).

Ride

The notation for the ride cymbal.

The largest of all the cymbals, the ride, is noted on the top black line (staff line 0). Just like other cymbals, the symbol to note the ride is an X with a stem.

Ride Bell

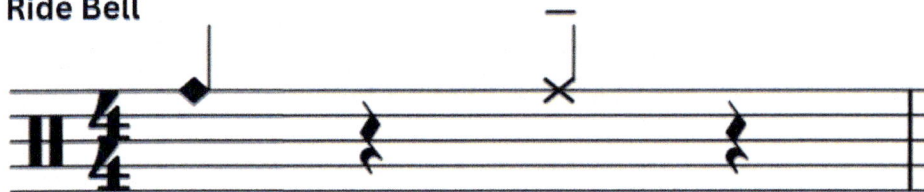

Ride bell   Crash ride

The notation for hitting the bell of the ride and hitting the ride cymbal as a crash.

The ride can be played in many ways from a gentle ping on the body of the ride cymbal, to using just the bell, or hitting it hard like a crash. The symbol for playing the bell of the ride is located on the same spot, but uses a little diamond instead of an X. The notation for playing the ride as a crash is the same as the regular notation for the crash, with a horizontal line added above.

Crash Cymbals

Crash 1   Crash 2

The notation for your first crash, and the second crash if you have one.

Crashes are located above the line of the hi-hat cymbal (staff line -2), written as an X with a stem like the other cymbals. The notation has a line running through it, as an imaginary line of the staff, to make it easier to distinguish from other lines. A second crash can be written above the imaginary line (staff line -3).

40

Splash Cymbals

Splash   Chinese cymbal

The notation for the splash and Chinese cymbals.

Less commonly used cymbals are the splash cymbal and the Chinese cymbal. Both are located on a second imaginary line above the regular staff lines (staff line -4). The splash cymbal uses the symbol commonly used for cymbals, whereas the Chinese cymbal is written using an X surrounded by a circle.

Alternative Drum and Cymbal Notation

You'll know that there are several different ways of playing a drum or cymbal. From rim shots to bell ride playing, this table provides an overview for the variations of some of the drum and cymbal notations.

Alternative Drum and Cymbal Notation

Drum/Cymbal	Drum Style	Staff Line	Notation
Snare Drum	Head	Staff line 3	
	Rimshot		
	Doubles (drum roll)		
	Buzz		

Ride Cymbal	Ride	Staff line 0	
	Bell		
Hi-Hats	Open	Staff line -1	
	Closed		
	Loose		

Hi-Hats	Pedal	Staff line 9	
Crash Cymbal	Hit	Staff line -2	
	Choke		

DRUM ACCENTS

Drumming isn't all about hitting drums and cymbals randomly,you've got to have control, panache, and flair. That's why accents can be used in drum notation.
Accents occur when you hit the drum or cymbal differently. It might be louder, quieter, higher, or lower. You might do a cymbal choke crash technique, where you grab the cymbal after hitting it, causing the crash sound to stop abruptly.

Types of Accents

There are lots of accent types in drumming that can be used for all sorts of drum music. These are four of the most common accent drum techniques:

The drag notation has small sixteenth-note symbols just before the note, with an underneath curve joining them.
Drag: The drag drum technique is created by striking the drum twice quickly with one stick followed by a single stroke with your other drum stick. It sounds like three notes played quickly together.

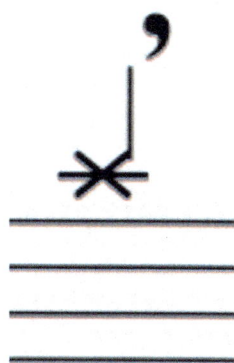

The flam notation is represented by a small note before a normal-sized note with a curved line underneath.
Flam: The flam drum technique is where you strike the drum with both sticks, with each strike slightly apart. It almost sounds like one note when played.

The ghost accent notation has a pair of brackets around the head of the note.
Ghost: Theghost note drum technique lightly plays bouncy notes on a snare drum that sounds like notes played in quick rhythmic succession.

The marcato notation has an upward-facing V symbol above it.

Marcato: Sometimes, you need to make a particular drum, cymbal, or snare loud and prominent in the song. The marcato technique just does that.

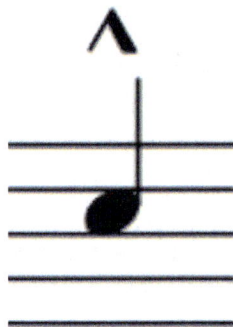

MUSIC NOTATION

Besides understanding drum notation, it is important to learn general music notation. This is because the music staff has other symbols and marks that help you read sheet music.

The Drum Notation Clef

The drum clef, followed by a 4/4 time signature.

The drum or percussion clef is a symbol at the beginning of the piece of drum sheet music consisting of two thick, vertical lines, which look like drumsticks. These tell you that this piece of music is yours to play. Sheet music with other clefs are to be used by other instruments.

Measures and Bar Lines

Measures usually consist of four beats and are separated by bar lines. Most of the time, measures will be separated by a single barline, although exceptions exist for showing repeats and jumps. The barlines contain your measures and beets, whichkeeps your sheet music organized and easy to read.

Time Signature

The time signature in drum notation is represented by two numbers, just like on other sheet music. The top number represents the number of beats in a measure, whereas the bottom number represents the note value of one beat. The most common time signature is 4/4, which has four beats per measure, where each beat is a quarter note. A more difficult example is ⅞, where each measure has seven beats, and each beat is an eight note.

Thetime signature is always written at the beginning of the sheet of music and at any point where a time signature change occurs throughout the music.

Different Length Notes

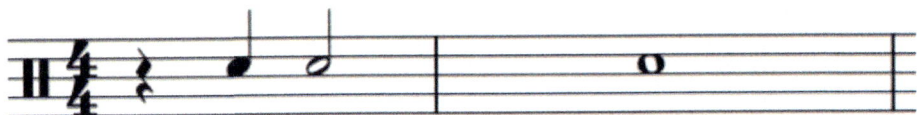

A quarter note, half note, and whole note.
It's not just the quarter note that appears in the measure. You can have longer notes, such as whole notes and half notes.

A quarter note, eight note, sixteenth note, and thirty-second note.
There are notes smaller than quarter notes as well, such as eighth notes, sixteenth notes, and even smaller fractions. The name indicates what fraction of a measure the length of the note is.

A triplet, where three notes are played in the duration of two.
Sometimes you can even have tuplets. These allow you to play a certain amount of notes in another timeframe. The most common type is the triplet, which tells you to play three notes in the space of two, and is indicated using a small '3' and a line linking the notes together.

Tempo

BPM (Beats per minute) or tempo tells you how fast you need to play the song. Having your metronome handy is crucial to get this locked in.

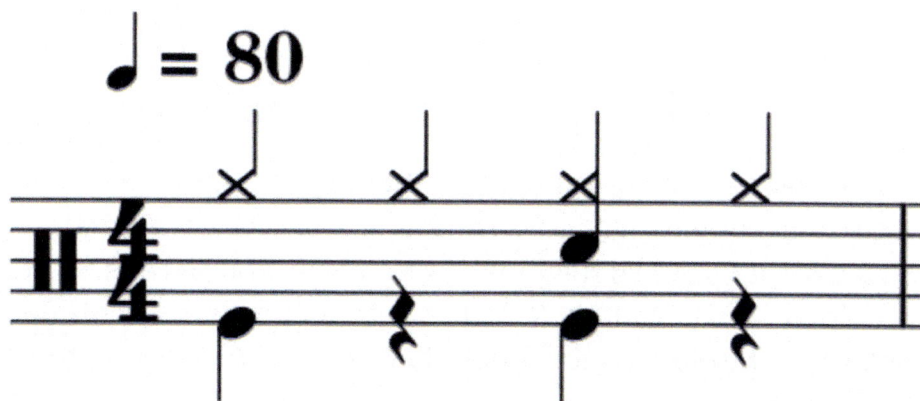

In the upper left corner the tempo of the song is shown. In this case, 80 beats, or quarter notes, per minute.

At the beginning of the drum notation sheet, you'll notice a note, usually a quarter note, with a number next to it.This tells you the Beats Per Minute (BPM) or Tempo. It shows you the note value, such as a quarter note, and how many times that note value gets counted in a minute.

Repeat Signs

As you well know, a lot of drumming includes the repetition of patterns and rhythms. Drumming sheet music recognizes this. So, to save space and avoid unnecessary complications, repeat signs are used. These tell you to play the same part again.

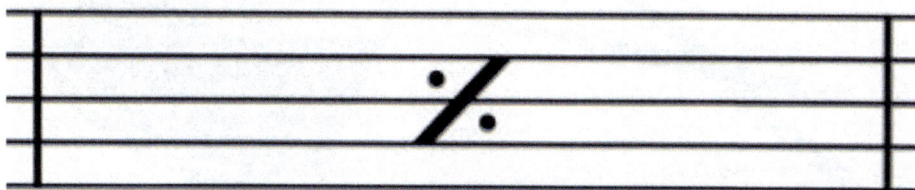

A one-bar repeat sign.
There are different repeat signs. The most commonly used is a one-bar repeat sign, indicated by two dots on either side of a diagonal line. It tells you to repeat the previous measure once.

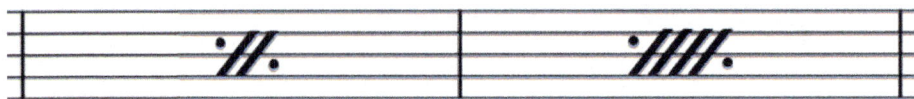

A two-bar repeat sign and a four-bar repeat sign.
A two-bar repeat sign looks the same as a one-bar repeat sign except with two diagonal lines. It tells you to repeat the previous two measures. A flour-bar repeat sign is sometimes used, which tells you to repeat the previous four measures.

TIPS ON HOW TO READ DRUM MUSIC

- **Take it slowly** - If you're just starting, it's okay to go slower than the set BPM. You can always speed up later. The technique comes first, tempo comes second.
- **Break it up** - Break the song into measures of 4, 8, or more. Focus on smaller parts of the song, so you can practice them repeatedly.
- **Repetition** - Do several 10- to 15-minute sessions on notation technique a day as part of your daily drum practice.

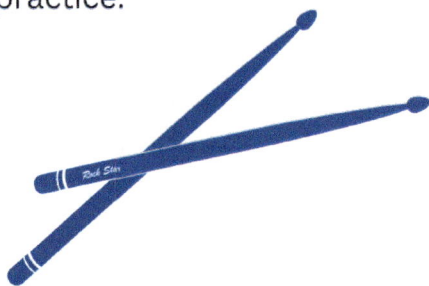

HOW TO READ DRUM TABS

Many drummers find tabs (short for 'tablature') the easiest kind of music to read. Tabs use Xs and Os to display drum and cymbal hits, and are usually ordered from the lowest sounding piece (the bass drum at the bottom) to the highest sounding piece (the cymbals at the top).

Like a simplified version of standard notation, drum tabs use a staff and legend. These are the basic abbreviations you'll see on tabs:

Drums (o)
- B, BD, or K: Bass drum/Kick drum
- S or SD: Snare drum
- T1: First tom
- T2: Second tom
- FT or T3: Floor tom or third tom

Cymbals (x or X [accented])
- H or HH: Hi-hat
- C or CC: Crash cymbal
- R or RC: Ride cymbal

```
H|  x  -  x  -  x  -  x  -  x  -  x  -  x  -  x  -
S|  -  -  -  -  o  -  -  -  -  -  -  -  o  -  -  -
B|  o  -  -  -  -  -  -  -  o  -  -  -  -  -  -  -
```

DIRECTIONS

Knowing how to read the road map is the key to a successful journey through any drum chart. Here are a few of the most common directional signs you'll come across:

Repeats

There's a lot of repetition in drum music, so you might see these a lot. A repeat is written as 2 vertical bar lines with 2 adjacent dots which signal that you should go back and play a section again.

"But where do I go back to?" Just look out for the inverted repeat sign to tell you the boundary of the repeated section. If there's no inverted repeat signal, go back to the beginning of the chart. Repeat the section once unless otherwise indicated.

First & second endings

Sometimes a section of your chart will repeat, but the last bar or two is slightly different each time. First and second ending markers make the whole thing easier to read by notating these varied endings without rewriting the entire section (so you'll ultimately have a shorter chart with fewer page turns).

The first time through, play the first ending (the measure with the "1" over it) and jump back to the inverted repeat sign. After you go through the second time, skip the first ending and jump directly to the second before you continue. Some charts have even more than two endings, so just keep repeating until you get to the last one.

Codas

This is another way to shorten the length of a chart by jumping backward and forward so you don't have to re-write a section that repeats. This concept can be tricky at first, but once you get it you'll be in great shape to read any kind of drum chart.

The first thing you'll need to look out for is the 'D.S.' or Dal Segno, which means "from the sign."

Think of this as a portal back to an earlier symbol in the chart (commonly called "the sign"). It looks like an 'S' with a backward slash through it and two dots on either side.

A 'D.C.', or Dal Capo is a similar concept that means "go back to the beginning" instead of to the sign. Either way, you're jumping backward to an earlier point in the chart.

Usually, the D.S. or D.C. marker will have the words "al Coda" or "al Fine" after it. This tells us whether to play straight through to the end ("al fine") or if we've got one more jump to make ("al coda"). If it's an "al coda," keep playing until you see a "To Coda" marker.

The Coda, which looks like a bullseye (or a circle with a plus sign in it), is our ultimate destination and the "To Coda" marker is another portal that sends us forward to get there (it's like warping in a video game). After you leap forward to the Coda, play through to the end and collect your prize.

Measure repeats & slash marks

These pop up a lot in drum charts. Full measure repeats are written as a backward slash with 2 dots and signal that you should play whatever you played in the previous bar. Multi-measure repeats will have 2 slashes and the number of bars written above this symbol.

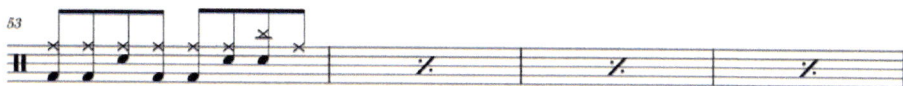

Many drum charts also use a concept called slash notation to indicate that the drummer should play time or continue grooving. This concept features crooked hash-marks on each beat of the measure instead of writing musical notation or patterns.

Compared to measure repeats, slash marks offer a bit more flexibility to vary the pattern you're playing.

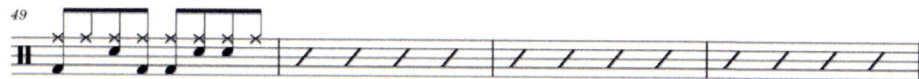

Measure numbers & rehearsal letters

Measure numbers are landmarks that tell you how many measures into the piece you are.

Rehearsal letters normally correspond with different sections of the song. The verse could be "Letter A," the chorus "Letter B," etc.

Both of these types of markers are especially useful when you're rehearsing longer pieces of music and usually appear to the left of the staff.

Lead sheets

These include the major landmarks of the song (like melody, dynamics, form and accents), and everyone in the band often reads the same one. These charts won't have the exact drum pattern written out for you, so the trick is to interpret the information and come up with the right groove, fills and other details.

Under Pressure

Queen/David Bowie

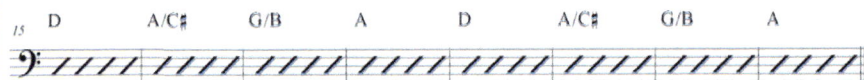

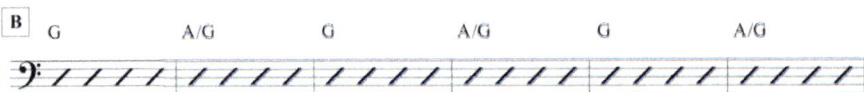

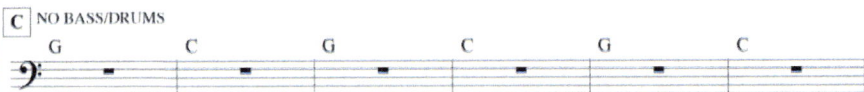

The more you encounter these charts, the better you'll get at using your ear and intuition to fill in the blanks.

BEGINNER DRUM LESSON

EASY ROCK DRUM FILLS

One of the toughest things about being a beginner rock drummer is coming up with drum fills that are easy enough to play.

On this page, you'll learn 7 basic rock drum fills and get fluent with the different parts of the drum kit. We'll cover the most popular fills used in rock music, which will act as the building blocks for advanced patterns you'll create in the future.

What's a drum fill, anyway?

Some drummers think a fill is the time to play a complex pattern or perform a miniature solo. While this is technically correct, a drum fill is meant to be a transition piece. You use it when you want to move to a different section in the song, such as from a verse to a chorus. Basically, a drum fill should be a deviation from what you're playing in order to introduce something new to the listener.

You can play a drum fill for as long as you want, but there are three common durations for fills that you'll hear regularly in rock music: the full bar (the longest), the half bar, and the quarter bar (the shortest). The main goal is to internalize the timing of these fills so you know when to start, and when to stop.

Most drummers will finish the fill with a crash, which marks the end of the transition and starts the next groove with a flourish on beat one.

> **Practice tip:** When going through these fills, try to practice them in phrases. This basically means just play a drum beat, play your fill, then go back to the drum beat. Act as if you were playing it within a song.

1. Nothing (we're serious)

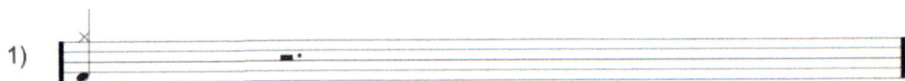

1)

"Wait... We're playing nothing for an entire bar?"
You'd be surprised how effective silence is at building tension. It's situational, but sometimes this is the perfect tool for the job. Go out on count one, come back in on count one. Boom.

2. The 8th note build

2)

This fill is known as the "8th note build". Start by playing 8th notes on the snare and floor tom at a low volume and slowly get louder at the fill goes on. This is called a **crescendo.**
Add in the bass drum on the quarter notes and you're ready to rip.

3. The 'dugga dugga'

3)

Arguably one of the most popular drum fills ever in rock music, this pattern consists of 16th notes all around the toms. You might think it's boring, but it's highly effective in this genre of music and perfect to start getting beginner drummers to explore the drum kit.

4. Bonham triplets

The famous Bonham triplet. We're moving from 16th notes to 8th note triplets

4)

(twelve notes per bar rather than 16 notes) for this drum fill. You can whip this puppy out in both straight and swung rock, making it a versatile pattern to have in your toolkit.

5. Half bar snare roll

5)

Our first half-bar fill! If you're looking for a quicker, more compact pattern to play that's not as intrusive as a full bar fill, start your fills on count three. This pattern consists of eight notes on the snare drum (alternating hands).

6. Flam fill

6)

Another popular "breakdown" style fill that's great for transitioning into another section in a song. The flam is a fun rudiment to incorporate into your fills, so try adding it into the other patterns on this list.

7. Quarter bar snare roll

7)

Lastly, let's talk about quarter-bar fills. These are perfect to toss in if you want to add some quick flavor, and they're subtle enough to duck under any vocal lines.

EASY DRUM SONGS

It can be tough to find songs to learn if you're just starting out on drums. Music that's too fast or complicated can be intimidating.

Here are 20 tunes in different styles to get you started. Each one has sheet music included, and some also have shorthand "road maps" that outline the form, hits and other important details in case you're still learning to read drum notation.

1. "Another One Bites The Dust" (Queen)

BPM = 110

This classic hit from 1980 is tons of fun to play on drums. The key is to keep a solid and steady backbeat on the snare throughout the whole tune. The bass drum plays every quarter note, which is called "four-on-the-floor."
The song begins with a "pickup" on the bass guitar, which means it enters just before the downbeat of the first measure when you'll play your first note. The verses and the choruses have the same pattern, so just keep chugging along!

Queen - "Another One Bites The Dust"
Album: *The Game* (1980) ~ Drummer: Roger Taylor
Transcription: Sergio Ponti

Verse 1
Chorus 1
Bridge
Verse 2
Chorus 2
Instrumental
Play 4x
4
Verse 3

Chorus 3

Guitar Solo

Outro

2. "Free Fallin'" (Tom Petty)

BPM = 84

Recorded in 1989 by Heartbreakers' drummer Phil Jones, this drum part is simple, but creative and grooving. Try to align your bass drum notes with the bass player, especially the "and" of beat 2 in each measure.

Verse 4 has a marching-style groove on the snare while the bass drum plays the same rhythm and the hi-hat foot plays 8th notes. This can be a real challenge to get organized, so practice slowly at first and stick with it!

Tom Petty - "Free Fallin'"

Album: *Full Moon Fever* (1989) ~ Drummer: Phil Jones ~
Transcription: Larry Crowe

♩ = 84 bpm

Intro

65

Interlude 2

Verse 4

Chorus 3

Interlude 3

Chorus 4

fade out

3. "Back in Black" (AC/DC)

BPM = 93

You can really rock out to this one. After the 2-measure intro, the full groove kicks in and you play 8 measures of groove before the vocals enter. Make sure to match your hits with the band in measures 6 and 10, and try not to rush them. Loosen your hi-hats for the choruses and make sure to nail those "Back in Black" hits with the vocals. This tune is over 4 minutes long, so try to keep the energy up the whole time.

AC/DC - "Back In Black"

Album: *Back In Black* (1980) ~ Drummer: Phil Rudd ~
Transcription: Hugo Janado

♩ = 93 bpm

Intro

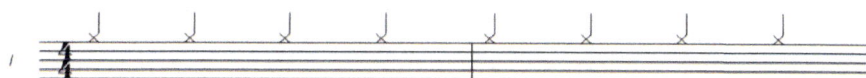

Verse 1 ("Back in black" ...)

Play hi-hats slightly open.

Chorus 1 ("'cause I'm back" ...)

("back in black"...)

Verse 2 (*"Back in black"* ...)

Play hi-hats slightly open.

Chorus 2 (*"'cause I'm back"* ...)

("back in black"...)

Guitar Solo

Chorus 3 (*"'cause I'm back"* ...)

("back in black"...)

Bridge ("'Ah, yeah" ...)

Chorus 4 ("'Well, I'm back" ...)

("back in black"...)

Outro

fade out

69

4. "Beast of Burden" (The Rolling Stones)

BPM = 102

This beat is vintage Charlie Watts: relaxed and perfect for the song. The intro pattern has some snare syncopation that matches the guitar part. Start by practicing that with just your hands, then add your feet.

The verses have a straight backbeat, but also make sure to emphasize those moments where he opens the hi-hats. Even a slight change in texture can make a big difference. The choruses are a constant build, with 8th notes on the bass drum creating momentum.

The Rolling Stones - "Beast Of Burden"

Album: *Some Girls* (1978) ~ Drummer: Charlie Watts ~
Transcription: Sergio Ponti

♩ = 102 bpm

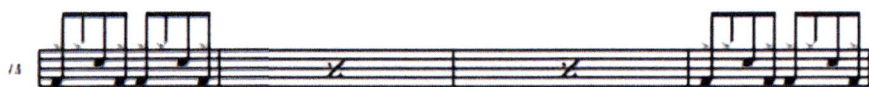

Chorus 1

Verse 2

Chorus 2

Bridge

Verse 3

Chorus 3

Outro

Thanks for Reading

Printed in Great Britain
by Amazon